# The Power of Patience

# The Power of Patience

Created by: Bro. Martin Edior

Edited by: Sis. Ethelinda Edior

**To order additional copies of this book, contact:**
Xlibris LLC
1-888-795-4274
www.Xlibris.com
Orders@Xlibris.com
90106

# The Power of Patience

Created by: Bro. Martin Edior
Edited by: Sis. Ethelinda Edior

| Library of Congress Control Number: | | 2010917574 |
|---|---|---|
| ISBN: | Hardcover | 978-1-4568-2309-2 |
| | Softcover | 978-1-4568-2308-5 |
| | Ebook | 978-1-4568-2310-8 |

This book was printed in the United States of America.

Rev. date: 11/19/2013

**To order additional copies of this book, contact:**
Xlibris LLC
1-888-795-4274
www.Xlibris.com
Orders@Xlibris.com
90106

# CHARACTERS

MAXWELL ...............................The father.

Suzette.....................................The mother.

Marvin.....................................The son. (age 10yrs)

Sue...........................................The daughter (9yrs)

Mr. Smithy ..............................The neighbor.

Mrs Smithy' wife

A Watch salesman

A purse and handbag salesman

A dancing-radio salesman

Four Professional dancers.

Dancer # 1

Dancer # 2

Dancer #3

Dancer #4

The Zebra Vicious Gang.
1$^{st}$ fella.
2$^{nd}$ fella.
3$^{rd}$ fella.
4$^{th}$ fella.

Police Officers.
1$^{st}$ officer.
2$^{nd}$ officer.

# ACT 1.

Scene 1.
The family is at the breakfast table.

The night is over as the sun slowly rises and the sounds of dogs barking in the distance, the birds are chirping and whistling on the tree tops, small animals like the squirrels are seen as they try to find something to eat, as they quickly climb the trunks of the nearby trees.

**SUZETTE** . . . . (As she now enters into the kitchen and goes to the stove, she puts on her frying pan and begins to fix breakfast as she hums a songs)

**MAXWELL** . . . . (As he now silently creeps up behind Suzette and grabbed her from behind as she howled in a surprised attitude. He turned her around and kissed her on the lips as he says) A very good morning to you my loving angel . . . . there seems to be sparks in your eyes this morning . . . . I wonder why?(as he chuckles)

**SUZETTE** . . . . (As she responds to his intimate kissing and replied) . . . . Well, my dear handsome fellow. It is all that tender loving that I received from you last night . . . . I must admit it was special-. (as she also chuckles and breaks away from his grasp.)

**MAXWELL** . . . . (Looking with love and admiration to his wife, then said,) Honey, may I help you in setting the table?

**SUZETTE** . . . . (As she glances over at him and smile) Sure, my love . . . . There is fresh orange juice which I made in the refrigerator, you can pour some into the glasses on the table, and the utensils are in the cabinet.

**MAXWELL** . . . . (He now goes to the refrigerator, takes out the juice, pours it into the glasses, goes to the cabinets takes out the plates, sauces, spoons, knives and forks as he begin setting the table for the family breakfast.

**SUZETTE** . . . . (she is busy frying the eggs and bacon attending to the toast in the toaster . . . . occasionally looking over at Maxwell and smiling at him as he is busy doing his duties.

**MARVIN** . . . . (As he now enters, yawning and scratching his head, rubbing his eyes . . . . He addresses his parents . . . . Good morning daddy, Good morning mommy . . . . (he goes over to his seat and sits down)

**MAXWELL** . . . . (looking at him curiously as he answers.) Good morning Marvin . . . . What is wrong with you? . . . .

**SUZETTE** . . . . (Also looking at him with concern as she also asked . . . .) What is it? Are you sick? Not feeling well? (as she walked over to him and put her arms around him)

**Marvin** . . . . (He straightens up and said . . . .) Well, l did not sleep too well last night . . . .

**MAXWELL** . . . . (Looking sternly at Marvin and asked-) And why was that, may l asked?

**SUZETTE** . . . . (Still standing there with her arms around him, looking gently down at him . . . . Yes, my son and how come you could not sleep? . . . . were you having bad dreams . . . .

**MARVIN** . . . . (As he looks up at his mother and quietly said) Well as soon as I felt asleep, I begin to feel the house shaking and a few books from my bookshelf felt off onto the ground, like an earthquake or something was rocking the whole house. (as he quiets down asking his mother) Mom was there an earthquake last night?

**SUZETTE** . . . . (As she quickly glances over to Maxwell and replied) Yes, my son, there was a small tremor, nothing too big to hurt any of us . . . . Your daddy and I are here to protect you and your sister in case of any huge earthquake . . . . Okay . . . . (as she kissed him on the cheek and said) Now get ready so we can have our breakfast . . . .

**MARVIN** . . . . Okay, mommy . . . (he looked at his father and said) Excuse me dad as I go to the restroom to wash up before breakfast . . . . (he gets up and leaves for the restroom)

**MAXWELL** . . . (Looking over at his wife with sneaky eyes, softly utters to her) Do you think he heard us last night?

**SUZETTE** . . . . (She walks over to Maxwell and kissed him as she replied) He is our son, 10 years of age . . . . He will soon grow up to be a man, so it is alright, whether he knows or not. I love you and we need to express that more often to our family, so they will grow up with the affection that they are learning from here at home and not on the street or other family's homes.

**MAXWELL** . . . . Yes, my loving angel . . . . I am the luckiest man in this world to have such an affectionate woman . . . (he again kissed her on the lips) And two loving kids . . . .

**SUZETTE** . . . . (She now breaks away from him and returns to the stove as she begins to dish out the breakfast in the plates)

**MARVIN** . . . (He returns to the table and sits down at his spot as he began a small talk with his dad) So Dad, were you frightened when the earthquake struck?

**MAXWELL** . . . (Looking at him with compassion, as he puts his arms around him and answered) Yes my son, your dad was a little afraid, but it is all gone now so let us not talk about it anymore o.k. We don't want to scare your sister. Right?

**MARVIN** . . . . O.k Dad . . . I understand, and where is Sue? (as he called out for her) Hey, Sue, where are you? . . . . It is breakfast time. You gonna miss it . . . .

**SUE** . . . . (now slowly strolling over to her chair and sits down as she looks at her father.) Hi Dad, Hello Mother . . . sorry I am late . . . . I did not sleep too well last night . . . .

**MARVIN** . . . . (As he anxiously looking at Sue when he bellows out and said) You too, felt the earthquake last night.

**SUE** . . . . (Looking at her mother and then to her father as she asked curiously) Mom, Dad, was there an earthquake last night? . . .

**MARVIN** . . . . (Before the parents could answer as they looked at each other, Marvin replied to his sister's question) Yes, Dad said, there was a small tremor and we should not be afraid, it is all gone, Right dad? (looking at his father as he sits there motionless).

**SUZETTE** . . . . (Addressing everyone at the table) Now settle down everybody, so we can have our breakfast and start a new day . . .

Suzette . . . NOW BEGINS TO SERVE THE BREAKFAST. SHE GOES OVER TO EACH PLATE AND SET DOWN THEIR PORTION AND SURPRISINGLY THERE WERE OBJECTIONS TO THE AMOUNT SERVED . . .

**MAXWELL** . . . . (Suzette goes over to his plate and placed on it a piece of bacon and one slice of toast he looks up at her) . . . . And what is this? Is this my breakfast, a piece of bacon and one slice of toast?

**SUZETTE** . . . . (She continues serving her breakfast. She takes up a long piece of bacon as she breaks it into two. She places one on Marvin's plate and the other on Sue's plate).

**MARVIN** . . . . (He quickly picks up the bacon and put it into his mouth and swallows it)

**SUE** . . . . (Calling out for her mother's attention and pointing to Marvin's plate) Mommy, mommy, look at Marvin's plate, he just gulped down his piece of bacon . . . .

**SUZETTE** . . . (She yelled at him) Marvin, how dare you? What kind of behavior is that,? (as she reaches over and spanked him on his wrist). Bad boy, and you will not get another piece.

**MARVIN** . . . . (after being quiet now) But mommy how come Sue has a bigger piece of bacon than mine . . . (looking down at his sister's plate)

**SUZETTE** . . . (looking over at his plate and replied) A bigger piece, eh, well young man, let's measure each piece to see whose is the biggest.

**MARVIN** . . . . (Realizing what he did) Okay Mom . . . I am sorry.

**MAXWELL** . . . . (He sits there observing his family as they chat around the table. He sips on his coffee, when he interrupted their conversion. OK, OK, kids, that is enough, your mom is doing the best she can. Let us try to work it out patience will get us through this little rough times . . . you will all see but we must have patience . . . Marvin, would you kindly say the grace this morning . . . (as they all bowed their heads in reverence).

**MARVIN** . . . . (Bowing his head, closing his eyes as he begins) . . . . "Dear Lord, please bless my daddy and mommy and my little sister and dear Lord please bless our table so we can have more food on our table next time, and a bigger piece of meat on my plate next time. Please look after my Daddy and Mommy as they go and come from work and look after me and my Sister when we go to school and on our way back to our home . . . Thank you Lord, we love you . . . . Amen . . . . Amen . . .

**SUZETTE** . . . . (As she looks at her son with admiration and said). Well done, son, that was awesome, wonderful . . . . (she reaches over and held his hands with delight)

**MAXWELL** . . . . (Looking over also at his son, Shaking his head) Well said, son and you deserve my piece of bacon. (as he picks up his piece and placed it onto his plate).

**SUZETTE** . . . . (Smiling, also at him with joyous expression said to him) And here is my portion of bacon also.(placing her piece on his plate)

**SUE** . . . (Sitting at her spot, remaining quietly, just looking on softly spoke and said to Marvin). Thank you Brother, that was a very good prayer.

**MARVIN** . . . . (All cheerful with all the praising from his parents, smiling as he says to his parents). Thanks Dad, Thanks Mom, and to you my little Sister how about this? (as he picks up the piece of bacon from his mother's portion and put it unto his sister's plate and puts his arms around her shoulders and says) I love you, Sis.

**SUE** . . . . (She looks over at Marvin and smiles and also replied) And I love you too, my big brother (as she squeezed his arm)

**MAXWELL** . . . . (Looking over to Suzette as he gives a big smile and says to her) . . . . And I love you too my dearest angel and you too Ms. Sue and Mr. Marvin . . . . I am the luckiest man in the whole world . . . . (as he laughs) . . . .

THE FAMILY CONTINUED THEIR BREAKFAST AS THEY CHAT AND LAUGHED UNTIL EVERYTHING THAT WAS PREPARED FINISHED . . . .

# ACT. 1.

Scene. 2.

## "THE DIAMOMD EARRINGS.

Well, the kids are off to school . . . Later in the day as Mr. Maxwell and Mrs. Suzette are sitting on the couch, holding hands chatting . . .

**MAXWELL** . . . Well dearest, we will have to come up with some type of plan to get over this little hard times we are facing. The economy is bad, no-one is investing as they ought to . . . . no new projects starting, no business hiring . . . no banks loaning any money . . . What are we going to do? (as he got up and walked to the window and looked outside, a little stressed)

**SUZETTE** . . . (As she remained sitting on the couch, sadly looking at her husband said,) I have been thinking too my love . . . but what can we do? Your company said they will re-hire you back as soon as business picks up (getting up and goes to her husband's side and holds his hands . . .)

**MAXWELL** . . . . (Turning around and hugging her) Yes, that is true, but no-one really knows when this recession will be over. This newly government administration needs to give it's citizens some type of financial assistance to help the economy back on the road. What do you think about that? (as he laughs out loudly) Ha, hah, hah, hah . . .

**SUZETTE** . . . (She also began laughing) Ha, hah, hah, hah . . . very funny, very funny . . . you think those government officials are thinking about their citizens . . . hah, hah, hah . . . (now walking away towards the refrigerator) Can I get you a beer, Honey? I think we only have one left . . .

**MAXWELL** . . . . (Looking at her with lovingly eyes, smiling as she steps towards the refrigerator) Yes, I would like a beer, if there is any left. And about these new government officials, I did vote for new Administration. The newly elected President made a promise to his citizens, that there will be changes and soon everything will be back to normal we just have to have a little patience.

**SUZETTE** . . . . (She returns with the beer and gives it to Maxwell) Yes, my darling. I have also voted for this new President, I like him and his whole family. I know in my heart that He will do good, especially with his loving, beautiful and talented wife as his coach . . . hah, hah, hah, hah. (as she laughs) And you are right everyone will just have to have a little patience.

**MAXWELL** . . . (Takes the beer out of Suzette's hands) . . . Thanks and don't you forget it too, my darling angel, that you, yourself are beautiful and talented and is my coach, so now what is my next move . . . . (as he giggles and kissed her on the lips)

**SUZETTE** . . . (She turns around after kissing and return to the couch and sat down with a can of soda in her hands) . . . .

**MAXWELL** . . . . (Looking curiously at her, as he followed and also sat down beside her and asked). What is it my sweetheart . . . What are you thinking? . . . . (putting his arms around her shoulders)

**SUZETTE** . . . . (She puts her can of soda down on the dining table, she began rubbing her face and eyes, and ears, when suddenly her hands touched her diamond-earrings. (She immediately jumps up with excitement in her voice) Max! Max, darling, darling, I have a brilliant plan . . . . (as she began gently caressing her diamond-earrings on her ears)

**MAXWELL** . . . . (little bewildered with Suzette's excitement remained sitting on the couch as he looks at his wife dancing around,) OK, OK, now what's with the excitement. I know, I just filled your head with all that good stuff, about being my coach and stuff, but what is going on in that little head of yours? (Getting up walking over to his wife).

**SUZETTE** . . . . (She is still thinking and still caressing her diamond-earrings on her ear)

**SUZETTE** . . . . (Now turned to her husband and says.) I have a plan, we do have a little money saved for emergency as you know, but with this plan that I have, (as she holds his hands) we will be able to get us ahead.

**MAXWELL** . . . . (Still does not have any clue about her plans asked very calmly) And may I asked what is your daring plan?

**SUZETTE** . . . . (She finally takes her diamond-earrings out of her ears while she was talking to Maxwell without him seeing her)

**MAXWELL** . . . . (Standing there, still sipping on his beer, calmly looking and waiting for her answer says) Well, are you going to tell me? . . . .

**SUZETTE** . . . . Yes, yes, yes, (she now shows him her diamond-earrings in the palm of her hands and said) . . . . Max, my love, these diamond-earrings could get us a great amount of money in town at one of the diamond stores.

**MAXWELL** . . . . (Shocked from seeing her diamond-earrings in the palm of her hands said) But Suzette, those are very special and precious to you. I cannot let you do that? Are you kidding me? No way! No way Those are your family emblem jewel, your great, great, great mamma's jewelry, I just cannot agree with this plan of yours. I just can't (as he puts down the can of beer on the table and walks a few steps away from Suzette sadly)

**SUZETTE** . . . . (A little stunned with his reactions, remained calm, looking at Maxwell as he stepped to the window looking outside she calmly walks over to him and puts her arms around his shoulders and whispers) I love you Maxwell, I love you very much, and I believe you, now you must believe in me. These diamond earrings are mine to do as I so please. Am I right?

**MAXWELL** . . . (Looking down at her and smiling a little) Yes my darling, they are yours to do as thou pleases. But they mean so much to you . . .

**SUZETTE** . . . . Yes, they mean a lot to me . . . but this is the time my mama told me, that if ever I ran into any financial difficulties, these diamond-earrings will bring you a fortune. So here we are, no food, no drinks, no work, what else to do {As she shows him her earrings)

**MAXWELL** . . . . But, darling . . . (taking the diamond-earring from her hands, said to her,) These look so beautiful on your ears.

**SUZETTE** . . . . Yes! Yes! They do look beautiful on my ears, but getting food and other necessities for my wonderful family is more beautiful than those diamond-earrings on my ears and besides I have extra ear-rings that I can wear. (as she kissed him on the cheek and walked to the kitchen. She opens the refrigerator and begin to fix something to eat.

**MAXWELL** . . . . (Standing there, holding the diamond-earrings in his hands, looking at his wife as she heads to the kitchen says) Honey, now these diamond-earrings are priceless, how much should I expect to get?

**SUZETTE** . . . . (Returning to him with a ham and cheese sandwich on a plate and puts it down on the table) OK, Max, sweetheart, let's eat as we discuss our plan. (they both sat down smiling at each other while Suzette sets the box for the diamond-earrings on the table).

**MAXWELL** . . . . (Sits down, bows his head, Suzette bows her head, as Maxwell prays). Dear Lord, we thank you for everything, my beautiful and charming wife, and two beautiful children, now dear Lord, this plan that my wife has created, so that we can get over this little hard times, we pray that you will make this plan works in Jesus Christ's name. Amen . . . .

**SUZETTE** . . . . (Looking up at Maxwell she smiled at him and said,) What a prayer? Thank you, it will work, only be patience as you go to town.

**MAXWELL** . . . . (Reaches over the table and kissed his wife, saying) Yes, yes, I know it will work. (he then picks up the diamond-earrings, and placed them into the box which Suzette had on the table).

**SUZETTE** . . . (Reaches over at Maxwell, and took his hands as she get up and walked over to his side of the table and said passionately) Well, Mr. Maxwell, Do you think that you could create another earthquake sequence before the kids get home from school. (As she giggles, pulling his arms as they head towards the bedroom).

**MAXWELL** . . . . Earthquake? Earthquake, what earthquake? (as he rolled his eyes . . . . then remembering his son's remarks at the breakfast, answers happily.) Oh, hell yeah, of course, earthquake, (as they both laughed and rushed into the bedroom, closing the door).

# ACT 2.

## "OFF TO THE MARKET"

Scene 1.

It is very early in the morning . . . Maxwell kisses his wife at the door, as he departed into town . . . .

**SUZETTE** . . . . (They embraced at the front door) Be careful, my darling, I love you. And remember, what ever situation you may encounter, remain calm and have lots of patience as our friend Job . . . (as she giggled)

**Maxwell** . . . (Kissed her on the lips) And, I love you too, look after the kids, well I will be back soon (as he departed, humming a tune glancing back at his wife as he got out of her sight).

**NOT VERY FAR AWAY HE SAW HIS NEIGHBOUR SITTING AT A BUS STOP ON A BENCH TALKING TO HIMSELF.**

**MAXWELL** . . . . (As he walked up to Smithy.) Hey Smithy, what is going on? Why are you out here, talking to yourself, like you are crazy or insane? What is happening to you and the wife? She still beating up on you? Ha hah, hah (as he sat down beside him)

**SMITHY** . . . . (Looking up and seeing his buddy) Hey, Max. boy you looking good, smiling and whistling. Where you off too?

**MAXWELL** . . . . Well, I am off to town to sell my wife's diamond earrings. Things are getting a little rough on my end. No food, no work. No money. I am not as fortunate as you inheriting all that money from your parents. And look at you still not happy. The wife still beating up on you . . . . hah, hah, ha, . . . (as they both laughed . . .).

**SMITHY** . . . . Nah, man, nah that is not so, she does not beat up on me. It is, like she is never satisfied with all the money I give her every week. She complains all the time that I do not give her enough, Boy . . . good for you your wife does not complain. Man you are the luckiest man around. (He looks at Maxwell . . . .) So you said, that you are going to town to do what?

**MAXWELL** . . . . . Yeah, man to sell these diamond-earrings of my wife. (as he reaches down into his pocket, takes them out and showed them to his friend Smithy)

**SMITHY** . . . (Looks at them with sparkles in his eyes) Man. Those are exquisite, they are gorgeous, beautiful . . . Man, they may be worth a fortune. I have never seen such diamonds like these before. How much do you think you can get for them?

**MAXWELL** . . . (Looking down at them also said,) Yes, yes, that is what I told my wife, but, the love for the family good and welfare was more important than the looks of these diamond-earrings, though I agree with you one hundred percent. As for the amount, I do not have the slightest idea.

**SMITHY** . . . . (Taking up the diamond-earrings in his hands, keenly looking them over,) How about I make a deal with you right here so that you do not have to go to town? (looking sternly at Maxwell).

**MAXWELL** . . . . (Rubbing his face, scratching his head, looking at Smithy) Well how much are you willing to give me?

**SMITHY** . . . (Looking more closely at the diamond-earrings, soon saw a an initial letter JM. inscribed very small within the jewelry as he shows it to Maxwell)

**MAXWELL** . . . . (He takes the diamond-earrings and looked at it closely) Yes, you are right, they are my wife's initial . . . Boy, you got very good eyes.

**SMITHY** . . . . Just, the same, now what about the price dear fella? (Taking back the diamond-earrings from his hands). These will look good on my wife's ears, that worthless wife of mine, but what can I say, I still love her very much, though she complains all the times . . . . hah, hah, hah, ha . . . . (as he laughs)

**MAXWELL** . . . . (Looking at Smithy) Hey Smithy, make me an offer?

**SMITHY** . . . . Well, since you are my friend and neighbor, I will give you one hundred dollars, cash right now, (he reaches down into his pocket and takes out a bundle of dollars and show him a hundred dollar bill) and here it is . . . .

**MAXWELL** . . . . (Looking at the bundle of bills in Smithy's hands and then over to the other hand with the one hundred bill,) What a friend? What a neighbor? All that money you have on you, this price-less diamond-earrings which you, said yourself worth lots of money, and you offer me, one hundred dollars . . . . boy what a pal!

**SMITHY** . . . . Well, why not? I was just testing you out to see if you will fall into desperation on your way to town . . . . (as he laughs out loudly.) Come on man, let's go to town, we have a pair diamond-earrings to sell Maxwell. (Also began laughing) You culprit, you're going to town with me . . . ha . . . ha . . . that is great . . . . but what about your complaining wife?

**SMITHY** . . . . (Looks at Maxwell) My wife, oh that is alright, she will just complain a little bit more but I am use to it and l still love her very much. Come, we must get to town before it gets dark . . . .

**MAXWELL** . . . . (puts the diamond-earrings back into his pocket as they take off singing and whistling a tune of some sort . . . .

# ACT 3.

## THE FIRST OFFER.

**Scene. 1.**

MAXWELL AND SMITHY SOON ARRIVE INTO TOWN. IT IS BUSY WITH ALL TYPES OF MERCHANDISE AND SALEMEN TRYING TO SELL THEIR PRODUCTS AND ITEMS. MUSIC PLAYING LOUDLY; PEOPLE SHOPPING,; LAUGHING; TALKING, EATING AND DRINKING . . . .

**MAXWELL** . . . . (all excited, looking here and there pointing to different stalls and items

**SMITHY** . . . . (Smithy whom is also excited). Yeah, yeah, yeah, and look over there at those lovely couches and chairs, and electronic items. (Also pointing out things to Maxwell) . . . .

**WATCH SALEMAN** . . . (shouting out his sales pitch) Watches, Watches . . . look at these beautiful watches. It alarms and rings out loud. Watches, get your bargain today. Now. Right now. (he looks at Maxwell) Hey, you over there! (pointing to Maxwell . . .)

**MAXWELL** . . . Looks at the watch-salesman and says) Who me ? (pointing to himself)

**WATCH-SALESMAN** . . . . Yes. You look like you are new to our shopping street. (as he goes towards Maxwell, and put his arm around him) Tell me what you are looking for? . . . . Look here I have beautiful watches, that I know your wife would fall in love with. (as he now shows him a few female watches) What do think? Aren't they gorgeous?

**Maxwell** . . . . (looking at the watches and feeling them around, still very excited with all the activities taking place all around him). How much is this one? (As he puts it on his wrist)

**WATCH-SALESMAN** . . . . Hey, fella. That looks great on your wrist. Well since this is your first time in town. I will let you have it for $20.00 dollars. How is that? . . . .

**MAXWELL** . . . Okay, that is great. I will take it. He puts his hands into his pocket, when suddenly he remembered that he had no money. (He turned around to look for his friend Smithy. (Smithy is no where around. He call out) . . . Smithy! Smithy! Smithy!

(The people began to look in his direction to see what is going on)

**WATCH-SALESMAN** . . . . (As he held Maxwell by his collar and said angrily) Hey, fella. What kind of trick are you trying to play on me? . . . . (He shakes him violently . . .) Now give me my $20.00 dollars before I kick your butt right here, you have me wasting my time and energy with you, come on man, give me my money (kept shaking him up)

**MAXWELL** . . . . (A little nervous, still looking around to see if he could see his friend Smithy) Listen, sir, I am telling you the truth, I do not have any money on me. I am going to the jewelry pawn shop so I could borrow some money on my wife's jewelry. (As he reached into his pocket, took out the box with the pair of diamond-earrings and showed it to the watch-salesman).

**WATCH-SALESMAN** . . . . (Snatches the box out of his hands) Here, let me look at those. Hey fella, not bad, they are gorgeous, man what A beautiful pair of diamond earrings, boy this is my lucky day. Now run along before I put a bullet in your butt. (He picks up his shirt and exposed the butt of his gun and you better not tell anybody or else, you will never make it back, wherever you came from. Do you hear me? (He shook him up a little more and kicked his butt). Now run along, and here is another watch for your wife. (as he gave him another watch)

**MAXWELL** . . . . (Took the watches, looked at them, saying out loudly to himself) Well, my two new friends, off we go, no need to worry about what happened here. (he puts his watches into his pockets) Well let's see what else is happening in town . . . . (he continues looking at the different stores and the items on display at the windows and side walks).

# ACT 3.

# THE BAG AND PURSE SALESMAN.

Scene. 2.

MAXWELL SLOWLY CONTINUES STROLLING ALONG THE BUSY STREET, WITH THE MUSIC PLAYING, KIDS RUNNING AND LAUGHING WITH THEIR FAMILIES . . . . VENDORS SHOUTING OUT THEIR PRODUCTS AND THEIR SALES BARGAINS.

**BAG AND PURSES SALESMAN** . . . . (He is waving a bag and a small flag to attract his customers . . . saying out loudly) . . . Bags! Bags! beautiful purses, lovely purses, just take a moment and see for yourself. Buy one get one free, come, come, the best deal in town, buy one, get one free.

**MAXWELL** . . . (Now arrives at the bag and purse salesman, as he stops and listened to him). Hello, sir those are beautiful bags and purses.

**BAG AND PURSE SALESMAN** . . . . (He goes to Maxwell with the bag and purse) Yes, they are, look, come into my store, there are many more selections that you can choose from. (As he hold onto Maxwell's hand and led him into his store) Come, come, many more for you to look at, you have a little time right . . . .

**MAXWELL** .... Oh yeah. Lots of time ... (he follows the bag and purse salesman into his store. He began to fumble around, looking at the different designs ... when he said to the salesman) Now I can touch and look but I do not have to buy anything, right? (As he remembers his first ordeal with the first salesman)

**BAG AND PURSE SALESMAN** . . . (.Putting his arms around Maxwell's shoulders) Sure my friend, you do not have to buy anything that you do not like . . . but I am pretty sure you will find something you like, take your time . . .

**MAXWELL** . . . . (Slowly walks around, looking at the different purses and bags when he picks up a set . . . matching bag and purse) Look here, sir a matching set . . . how much may I ask? (looking at the salesman, smiling) I love those, my wife will be pleased with these . . . .

**BAG AND PURSE SALESMAN** . . . Well, you seem to be a kind-hearted fellow, how about $25.00 dollars, and remember the deal you get to pick another item.

**MAXWELL** . . . . Oh yeah, but sir, I really love this matching sets, but I do not have any real money on me at this moment . . . .

**BAG AND PURSE SALESMAN** . . . . (He gets closer to Maxwell) What do you mean, you do not

have any real money on you? What do you have then?
(Looking at him curiously)

**MAXWELL** . . . . (Reaching into his pocket, takes
out the two watches, (he had received from the first
salesman and showed them to him) Here, these two
watches I have which I am going to the jewelry pawn
store for a loan. (He gives them to the salesman)

**BAG AND PURSE SALESMAN** . . . . (Takes the
watches and looked them over, puts them to his ears
as he listened) Yeah, yeah, they work . . . I like the
ticking sounds. Okay fellow, lets make a deal . . . You
said that you like the sets which you hold in your
hands . . . right?

**MAXWELL** . . . . (Looking at the sets in his hands)
Yes, l do,

**BAG AND PURSE SALESMAN** . . . . Okay, here is
the deal, you can pick another set of bags and purse
and I get to keep these watches how is that? A deal
or not! . . . (he goes over and placed his arms his
shoulders, he stretched out his hand to Maxwell as he
shook it.)

**MAXWELL** . . . . (Stretched out his hands and shook
the salesman's hands and said out vibrantly) It is a
deal! . . . . (as they both began laughing) Ha, hah.
Ha . . . Thank you. (as he continued on his journey).

# DANCING RADIO SALESMAN

## Scene 3.

Maxwell with his bags and purses continues on his journey. He is enjoying himself, he would make a few dancing steps from time to time as the music continued to play in the market place.

**MAXWELL** . . . . (Speaking out loudly . . . .) I wander what happened to Smithy, my friend . . . boy I hope he is alright . . . his wife will never forgives me if anything bad should happen to him. It is because of me he came along and now, I don't even know where he strolled off to . . . . (he looks up and saw people dancing to disco music . . . . laughing and dancing away . . . it was a break dance party . . . . He hurried to the scene, standing by and observing the different dancers as they took turns in performing their styles and talent)

**THE DANCING RADIO-SALESMAN** . . . . Listen up fellas . . . . this is the way it will be . . . . we will have a break-dancing contest . . . . the winner will get this gigantic box radio here with a dozen of disco C.D'S. to play along . . . .

**MAXWELL** . . . . (Standing with the rest of the people listening to the Radio-salesman, now steps up to him saying) . . . . Hello sir, I would like to compete for your radio and C.D.s.

**DANCING RADIO-SALESMAN** . . . . Okay sir, what is you name?

**MAXWELL** . . . . My name is Maxwell.

**DANCING RADIO-SALESMAN** . . . . Okay Maxwell, stand over there.

**DANCING RADIO-SALESMAN**. (As he calls out to the crowd gathering)

Let's see if there is anymore dancers in the crowd. (he shouts) Any more dancers who want to win this grand radio with the latest C.D.S. to go with it? Come on lets break-dance a little, let's show the town folks what break-dancing is all about . . . .

(Suddenly there were voices as they came on the platform that the Radio-salesman had prepared for this contest . . .)

1$^{st}$ professional dancer . . . . (he steps forward) I would like to dance too.

2$^{nd}$ professional dancer . . . . (steps forward) I would like to join them also

3rd professional dancer . . . . (he steps forward) Don't leave me out.

4th professional dancer . . . . (he steps forward) Count me in. I am down.

**DANCING RADIO-SALESMAN** . . . . Okay dancers, this is the way it will work, to win this big fancy radio with the music to go with it . . . each one of you will have to pay a fee of $5.00 dollars to compete . . . .

THE FOUR DANCERS PAID THEIR FEE TO PARTICIPATE IN THE DANCE CONTEST, WHEN HIS TURN CAME UP TO PAY . . . HE TELLS THE RADIO-SALES MAN.

**THE DANCING RADIO-SALESMAN** . . . . Hello Maxwell. Let me have your $5.00 dollars . . . . (he advances to him with outstretched hand to get his money . . . .

**MAXWELL** . . . (Shaking his head- . . . as he said to the radio-salesman) Sorry sir, I don't have any money on me right now . . . but if you will allow me to dance in your contest, I will pay you back after I trade off these purses and bags for money.

**THE DANCING RADIO-SALESMAN** . . . . Bags and purses! (replied the radio-salesman) . . . . Where is the bags and purses?

**MAXWELL** . . . . (He showed the items to him) Here they are sir.

**THE DANCING RADIO-SALESMAN-** . . . Ok, good let me have them . . . consider your fee paid up. Prepare to break-dance . . . . (he stepped off the platform as he announces) Let the music play . . . and dancers you have 5 minutes to empress everyone looking on here and to take home the grand prize this F.M.AM. STEREO TYPE SYSTEM, with CD and cassette player . . . Let the contest begins.

1st professional dancer stepped on the platform . . . . (he did his styles and tribute to the break-dancing community) . . . .

2nd professional dancer stepped on the platform . . . . (does his thing, the crowd builds him up with his style) . . . .

3rd professional dancer stepped on the platform . . . . (also made some fanciful break-dancing movements) . . .

(Again the crowd went wild as they enjoyed the fun with all the different strokes from the different dancers)

4th professional dancer . . . (steps forward, stopped turn around and beckoned Maxwell to join him on the platform)

**MAXWELL** .... (Hurried on the platform as they both began to break-dance, they were really having a good time. The people all around the nearby stores began to assembled to watch the dancing contest. The music is blasting, disco style. The dancers are dancing . . . the crowd is dancing, everyone was now dancing where they were standing when suddenly . . . .

**MAXWELL** .... (He howled out on the platform) My heart, My heart, my heart .... ooohhhh (as he slowly fell to the ground)

Everyone stopped dancing, the music stopped playing. People began walking away from the area .... the professional dancers all slipped away . . . .

**MAXWELL** ... (now lying on the platform by himself)

**THE DANCING RADIO-SALESMAN** .... (rushed over to where he was lying motionless.) Oh, my Lord! Oh my Lord! (he immediately lifted his head and began to fan him, then he began performing cpr on him.

MAXWELL .... (As he grasped for air as the salesman performed on him . . . Looked up and smiled) What happened?

**THE DANCING RADIO-SALESMAN** .... I think the dancing fever was too great for your heart, it couldn't take all the turning and twisting you were doing, ha, trying to keep up with that young fellow nearly killed you . . . . (they both laughed)

**MAXWELL** . . . . (He gets up and looking around, he sees no-one) . . . What happened to everyone?

**THE DANCING RADIO-SALESMAN** . . . . Oh, they all went on with their businesses. They did not want to be involved if you had not regained your strength. Anyway, you had the right movements to gain my vote, so here is your prize and your bags and purses, enjoy the rest of your journey Maxwell, it was nice knowing you and here is a lunch box with some food, water and cookies for the rest of your journey . . .

**MAXWELL** . . . . (He thanked the radio-salesman). Well, thank you very much sir, for returning the purses and bags . . . these are for my wife and daughter (he shook the salesman's hand and continued on his trip.)

# ACT 3.

## MAXWELL CONFRONTS
## THE ZEBRA GANG.

**Scene 4**

Maxwell, leaves the dancing platform, saying good-bye to the radio-salesman . . . . as he continues his journey, he looks up ahead and sees a large oak tree on a hill not far away as he said out aloud) . . . . Boy I could use a little rest. (he hurries up to the oak tree.)

**MAXWELL** . . . . (Boy, oh boy, what a trip. I am tired, I need to rest awhile here before I continued. (he gets under the oak tree, sits down and opened the lunch box that he received from the last salesman . . . .) he drinks the water, eats the cookies and the sandwich which was in the box. (he yawns as he says,) Oh no, I feel drowsy, I must take a little nap. (as he lay down to rest immediately he fell asleep. He began snoring out loudly) . . . .

**THE ZEBRA GANG NOW WAS ON THE PROWL. THAT OAK TREE WAS THEIR CENTRAL MEETING PLACE-. AND NOW IT WAS TAKEN BY A STRANGER WHO WAS FAST ASLEEP, SNORING AWAY . . . .**

**1ˢᵀ Gang member-** . . . . Look padres, look up yonder, there is a guy lying in our territory, is he insane or mad . . . . that is our turf . . . . come on let's see who this gringo is . . . we gonna kill him . . . . (they began laughing. (they all hurried up to the oak tree quietly, looking at Maxwell, as he was sound asleep . . .)

**2ⁿᵈ Gang member** . . . He picks up a small twig and pass it on his nose . . . . they smiled as they played little tricks on him as he slept.

**MAXWELL** . . . . (Not aware of the gang's presence, wiped the twigs that was lying on his face, as he turned over and fell back to sleep)

3ʳᵈ Gang member . . . . Boy this guy is a heavy sleeper, (he now looked over to the music box which was playing, he picked it up and puts it close to Maxwell's ears as he turned it on with the full volume- . . .)

**MAXWELL** . . . . (Suddenly gets up and saw the gang surrounding him . . . .) He stood up, (he addressed the gangs) Hello fellas . . . how you guys doing?

**4ᵗʰ Gang member-** . . . . (stepping forward in front of Maxwell, looking straight into his eyes.) How are we doing? You gently asked. Well for one thing we are not doing too well, and you are trespassing. Hey, man you are on our turf, and there is a big price for invading our sacred grounds.

The rest of gang began to surround Maxwell .... poking him and slapping him around with their hands ....

**MAXWELL** . . . . (He tried to defend himself by saying,) Ok guys! I am sorry, I am leaving right now, no need to get violent ....

**1ˢᵗ Gang member** .... (Jumping in front of Maxwell) Violent, eh violent, did you say violent, well buster, that is our middle name .... How did you know? ... (as he punched him in his stomach ...).

**MAXWELL** . . . . (He stumbled back with the pressure of the 1st gang's punch to his stomach). Okay, fellas, I said I am sorry, now let me go my way, no-one will get hurt. OK. now come on guys. What's the problem here?

**2ⁿᵈ Gang** .... Well sir, the problem here is you have to pay us for sleeping under our oak tree(They began laughing and punching him)

**MAXWELL** .... Pay you for taking a nap under this oak tree .... That is against the law. Isn't it? You guys are crazy, paying you for taking a nap. (Begins to walk away ....

**3ʳᵈ Gang member-** ... Yep! fella, we are the law around here, so stop the bullshit, take out all your money from your pockets and give it to us right here and now, no more bullshit, (as he gave him a blow to his jaw a right and left blow with his fist)

**MAXWELL** . . . . (Gets the blow from the 3rd gang fist and falls backward on his back he howled out in pain). Oh my God! Oh my God! (he quickly got up and prepared himself for a fight, he looked around and picked up a large piece of timber from the oak tree. He now advances to the Gang . . .) Okay, okay, I told you guys to walk away, but you insist on messing with me . . . well come on let's see who is the toughest fellow among you . . . . robbing innocent people around your town. Come on let's do it.

**4th Gang member-** . . . (looking at his buddies, as he nods to them to rush him . . . . but his guys did not understand his signal and so when he rushed Maxwell, Maxwell took the large timber branch and whack, whack, on his head as he fell down on the ground and fainted, Maxwell whack him a few more times as he laid motionless on the ground . . . .

**3rd Gang member** . . . . (seeing one of their fellow got whack and passed out, howled out.) Get up man! get up man! (He now tried to rush Maxwell)

**MAXWELL** . . . (Again moving sideways, as the gang fellow missed him, Maxwell spun around and smack, smack on the back of the 3rd gang member's neck, he too felt down howling out in pain and fainted . . . .

(Maxwell, quickly advanced on him and give him another blow on his head . . . as he too remained motionless.)

**1ˢᵗ gang member**-(. . . looking at his buddies remaining and said to him . . . .) Man too hell with this fellow, I am leaving I am going for more help as he turned and ran away . . . .)

**2ⁿᵈ Gang member**- . . . . Looking at Maxwell, (Maxwell, still holding onto his timber limb, looking sternly at the 2nd gang member,) Listen Mister, I am very sorry if we made you mad . . . . I am not really a gang member, but these guys made us join their gang, and if we did not join their gangs, then they would beat us up and our families . . . That is the way in this part of the town . . . .

**MAXWELL** . . . . Okay, little man, I accept you apologies, now run along.

**2nd Gang member**- . . . Thank you sir, (as he took of running behind his buddy, shouting) Wait, wait, for me wait for me, I am coming . . . . I am coming.

**MAXWELL** . . . (Looking at the young man running down the hill . . . He now goes over to the fallen gang members . . . . he shook one first, then the other, he then emptied their pockets, as he goes through their pockets, he now heard voices coming to him . . . he looked up and here comes more gang members . . . .

He quickly got up and picked up another piece of timber nearby and stood firm, with one fist cling ready to fight for his life.)

1st **gang member**-(He advanced to Maxwell), Hey fella, you think we would let you walk away from here so easily! . . . . come on now, let's see what type of fighter you really are . . . .

2nd **Gang member** . . . . also walked up to him laughing . . . ha . . . ha . . . sorry sir, now fellas, as he instructed his buddies to rush Maxwell . . . . They all rushed him at the same time, as they crushed him, (he was powerless, he was no match for them . . . they began to beat him up) . . .

**MAXWELL** . . . . The gang rushed him together and so they all fell on him as he hits the ground, they began punching him and beating him with the timber he had in his hands . . . He howled out in pain, help, help, someone help as he cried out in agony and pain . . . . 1st and 2nd gang now hold him down . . . . See what he has in his pockets . . . . (they looked into his pockets . . . .) they found nothing

2nd **gang member**-(he tells his other buddies) Okay, fellas, get the radio, the bags, the purses and the

C.D.s and get those two jokers lying over there on the ground, shame on them letting this guy whack them like that. Okay, let's scram out of here, they all ran off laughing ha, ha, hah, hah, hah . . . . ho, ho.

**MAXWELL** . . . After a few moments, badly beaten, busted lips, black eye, swollen body parts, he slowly got up and made his way back to the town.)

It is now late in the afternoon, most of the town folks have gone home, most of the vendors and salespeople have closed up their businesses . . . .

**MAXWELL** . . . . (Slowly stumbled along the path towards home, he mutters somethings to himself). What am I gonna do? Everything I had I lost . . . my friend ran away from me, my wife's diamond earrings, I lost, the watches, I lost. The bags and purses, I was robbed and on top of everything, I almost lost my life . . . . (he looked up to heaven as he howled out) What next Lord.? How much more patience can a man bear? (he sat down on a bench nearby groaning in pain, as blood sipped down his cheek from the blows he had received from the gangs . . . . He stretched out on the bench, as he rested for a while closes his eyes and said) Oh well, I did try, sorry my love. My patience runs out. (wounded and tired from his conflict with the gang, he fell asleep on the bench, as drops of blood dripped down the side of his face . . . .)

# ACT 4.

## THE CONCERNED FAMILY.

### Scene 1.

At home, Suzette was preparing dinner. The kids were on the couch, looking at the television . . . .

**SUE** . . . . (She got up from the couch and goes to the kitchen) . . . Mama, I wondering what happened to daddy, it is getting very late. Do you think anything has happened to him? . . . .

**SUZETTE** . . . . (Looks around at her daughter, goes to her and hugged her) Oh no, my precious, your daddy is a fighter, he was a professional boxer before l married him. He stopped fighting after l gave birth to you my princess, because of you . . . Daddy loves us very much . . . He is ok.

**MARVIN** . . . . (Now joined in as he too went into the kitchen) Really, mamma, daddy was a real professional boxer . . . . wow! my daddy a boxer, wow !.

**SUE** . . . Boxer or not, if three or four bad men rush up on him together, he will not be able to fight them off.

**SUZETTE** . . . (Getting a little angry with her daughter's nagging opinion on her father's welfare.)

now stop this talk and get back and look at your television as I get our dinner ready ok sweetheart, daddy will be alright. (give a small kiss on her cheek as she left).

**MARVIN** . . . . (Looking at his sister and said,) It is alright little sis, Daddy will soon come home, you will see, now come let's go back and look at our television. Ok.(also kissed her on her cheeks)

**SUE** . . . . (As she blushed when her brother kissed her on the cheeks and answered . . . . Okay. (they both returned to the couch.)

**SUZETTE** . . . . (She finished fixing dinner, she sets the table and then joined the kids on the couch . . . . What are we watching?

**MARVIN** . . . . (He answered . . . . Discovery channel . . . . mama . . . . there is so much to learn from this channel . . . .

**SUZETTE** . . . . (She reaches over and pat him on his shoulders . . . Excellent my son . . . good choice . . . .

**MARVIN** . . . . Mama, why did daddy had to go to town?

**Suzette** . . . . Well, son, we were out of groceries and other stuff, and so your father had to go to town to buy us those things for the house . . . . He usually gets home a little after sun-down . . . . He should be back very soon . . . (they all kept on viewing the television)

## ACT 5

## MAXWELL REUNITES WITH SMITHY.

**Scene. 1.**

Maxwell, lying on the bench, groaning in agony from the beating he received . . . tries to get up but only cries out more louder . . . .

**MAXWELL** . . . . OOUCH . . . . OOUCH . . . OOH OOH . . . . (As he mumbles) Boy what trouble I am in . . . . no money. no diamond-earrings, no nothing (as he bellows out) and my God, what will I tell my wife and kids when I return home . . . Oh no,(as he cried out and tears ran down his cheeks . . .)

He slowly tried to get up when he heard whistling sounds getting closer and closer . . . . he looked up and began to whistle the same tune also . . . .

**SMITHY** . . . . (Hearing the whistling sound also as he approaches the bench, he looked up and there was his friend Maxwell lying down groaning in agony and pain. He stopped whistling and now hurried to his friends side) . . . Max, Max, man what the franc happened to you . . . Oh my heavenly father! (looking more closely, as the blood still dripping down his face/) Smithy now helps Maxwell to sit up) Took out his handkerchief, opened up his bag that he was carrying along, got some water, and attended to Maxwell's wound.

**MAXWELL** . . . . (Very happy to see his friend and neighbor, held unto him as he sobbed a little) Sorry dear old boy, I am sobbing because I thought something bad had happened to you, and what will I tell your complaining wife . . . . (they both laughed a little as he let him go) he dried his tears and they began to chatting . . . .

**SMITHY** . . . . (Looked at sadly at Maxwell and asked) so what happened? Who did this to you?

**MAXWELL** . . . Well, when we arrived here early this morning I was attracted to a watch-salesman and I began looking over his stuff. They were very good looking stuff, so I found one that I had loved, but after taking up the salesman time, I then realized that I did not have any money to pay him . . . . So I looked around thinking you were with me, also looking at the watches but you were gone. I even called your name out loudly a few times . . . but no answers buddy . . . .

**SMITHY** . . . . Yeah, and so what happened,?

**MAXWELL.** Well, what do you think happened? . . . . the fellow wanted to beat me up and he even show me his gun . . . so I had to trade my wife's diamond earrings for two watches.

**SMITHY** . . . . (Got angry.) You mean you traded off your wife's precious diamond earrings for two lousy watches Man. Max, you are mad! very mad! how could you? . . . .

**MAXWELL** . . . . Calm down Smith, boy, if you were in my shoe, you would have had no choice but to comply . . . . believe me buddy, believe me, I had no other choice . . .

**SMITHY** . . . . (returned and sat down besides his buddy . . .) Okay and then what happened?

**MAXWELL** . . . I had two more amazing incidents, at one of them, I had fainted, and a good fellow revived me back to life . . . . then I decided to rest under an oak tree before I continued a little further into town when a bunch of young hoodlums jumped me and took all my stuff and beat me up . . . .

and here I am, broke, and even more broke than when I last saw you . . . . (as he tried to laugh but could not because of his pain) but tell me about your adventure . . . .

SMITHY . . . . Yep, mine was a happy and joyous adventure . . . no pain, no buying and selling stuff. You remember the first store with the watches and stuff.

**MAXWELL** . . . . Yeah, that is where I lost you.

**SMITHY** . . . . Well, just across the other side was a charter bus which says free ride to the horse-racing track, so I immediately got into the bus as it took off . . . . I try to wave at you but you were too busy with the watch-salesman, so I kept on going . . . .

**MAXWELL** . . . . . (He pats Smithy on his shoulders . . . .) Yeah buddy it is alright, at least you are safe, and I am a little wounded but everything will be alright . . . (he groans in pain) it is my arm, I think it is fractured from the punching and boxing with those gang members.

**SMITHY** . . . . But wait, Max, you haven't heard all the great news . . .

**MAXWELL** . . . Yeah . . . . great news eh . . . . you won a few thousand of dollars eh . . .

**SMITHY** . . . . (As he laughed out loudly) . . . . ha . . . ha . . . ha . . . ho . . . ho . . . My friend are you a prophet of some kind . . . . you are absolutely right, I won $25,000.00 dollars in cash.

**MAXWELL,** (Looking at Smithy surprisingly and said) Now wait a minute. I was only joking, you mean you really won $25,000.00 dollars

**SMITHY** . . . . Hey buddy, would I tell you a lie . . . (as he picked up the bag he was carrying and tossed out it's contents, and out flows hundreds of dollars as it dropped to the ground . . . .

**MAXWELL** . . . (All excited, immediately jumped off the bench and begin to touch the bills and played with the hundred dollar bills, as he smelled them and tossed them around, as if they were his . . . . He was happy, he no-longer was in pain)

**SMITHY** . . . . (Also was very happy, as he looked at his friend playing with his money when he said to Maxwell . . . .) Well max, boy we have some money in our midst, and if it was not for you inviting me to tag along, I would not have won this money . . . so what are we gonna do with this here money? . . .

MAXWELL . . . . (Sat down on the ground with all the dollar bills around him . . . he was dazed with joy, he no longer felt the pain, the joyous moods revived the pains and agony from his beating) Then he looked at Smithy and said,) Well dear Smithy, it is your money, and I cannot tell you what to do with it. (looking at Smithy with a smile,)

SMITHY . . . . Okay . . . I have a plan . . . . listen to this . . . . I will share half of this money with you, if you can prove to me that when you get back home, your wife will not be extremely angry with you for losing her diamond-earring . . . .

**MAXWELL** . . . . (Looked up at Smithy as he sat on the bench) He got up and limped over to the bench and sat besides him . . . .) Okay, now tell me your plan again . . . . I am listening now, before, I was too far, come again . . . (as he laughed out discreetly)

**SMITHY** . . . . Ok, I said, that I am willing to give you half of all this money lying here in front of us if your beautiful and loving wife do not get extremely mad with you for losing her diamond-earrings.

**MAXWELL** . . . . Alright, it is a bet . . . but how would you know if she gets angry or not? (as he now looked at Smithy)

**SMITHY** . . . . Well, let see here, for one thing you will have to sneak me into your closet . . . .

**MAXWELL** . . . . Into my closet, (he yelled out) . . . Are you insane man? Into my closet! how dear you? . . . peeping tom, eh, Smithy, is that what you want?

**SMITHY** . . . (As he jumped away from Maxwell's responds) Oh no, oh no Max, I don't mean it like that, no sir, not at all, the way you are thinking, it is wrong. Now listen carefully . . . don't get angry, just listen carefully, now you said to me that you have a loving and grateful wife, right, she believes in you and that patience conquers everything, we learned that from the Holy Scriptures the story of Job . . . Right! okay now all I am saying to you, is I will only be in the closet for a brief moment, only when I am convinced that your wife is not angry with you for losing her diamond-earrings. What is so bad with that? Hey take a look at all this money lying here, half could be yours. What are you saying? (as he began laughing, and as Maxwell also began laughing) ha, ha, ha,

**MAXWELL** . . . (Looking at Smithy) Okay man, it is a bet. I will prove to you that my wife is not about material things, like other women. Come let's try to get home before it gets too late, my wife and kids get pretty worried at this time when they don't see me come home at a certain time. (he slowly got up as Smithy helped him to steady himself)

**SMITHY** . . . . (As he gathered up the money and put it back into the bag) he helped Maxwell unto his shoulders) and said, hold on to me Max, come on old fart, we are going home (as they giggled on way home).

**MAXWELL** . . . . Hey smith, what you just called me, old fart?, Boy watch your mouth you old fart yourself . . . (they both began laughing as they began whistling their favorite tune . . . . they slowly head for home.

# ACT 6.

## MAXWELL'S FAMILY PREPARES TO GO AND FIND THEIR FATHER

**Scene 1. . . . .**

It was after dust, the sun had set long ago, it was close to 9pm . . . the Maxwell's family was getting very worried . . . . and quite concerned . . . .

**SUZETTE** . . . (She looked at her kids as they sat solemnly on the couch) as she said to them . . . . Listen kids, I know that daddy is alright, he is just taking his time in returning, maybe he was tired, and took a nap under some big tree, and overslept. You know stuff like that could happen.

**MARVIN** . . . Yes mama, but what about if he does not get up, then what?

**SUZETTE** . . . . Well, that is a good point there son, do you have any suggestions?

**MARVIN** . . . Yes mama, let us all get ready and go in search for our daddy. He might be hurt and lying somewhere wounded. (as he looked at her)

**SUE** . . . . (Also got up from the couch and hurried into her room, as she yelled) hold on daddy, we are coming! We are coming!

**SUZETTE** . . . (Goes to the table and clasped her hands in prayers, closed her eyes and begun to prayer . . . . Dear Lord of tender mercies, and loving care, look upon my daring and brave husband, protect him from any danger that may try to hurt him and dear Lord return him to us safely, please in Jesus Christ's name . . . Amen . . . .

MARVIN AND SUE CAME TO THE TABLE QUIETLY AS THEIR MOTHER WAS PRAYING WITH HER EYES SHUT FOR HER HUSBAND'S SAFE RETURN. BUT WHEN SHE OPENED HER EYES SHE SAW THEM ALSO PRAYING THEN SHE REACHED OVER AND EMBRACED THEM.

**SUZETTE** . . . Okay, my children, remain here as I run over to Mr. Smithy's home to ask if he will come along with us to find your father. Go to your rooms and remain quiet and do not come out until, I call out for you. Is that clear to both of you?

**MARVIN** . . . Okay moms (he looked at his sister and took her by her hands as they left for his room)

**SUZETTE** . . . . (Took up a baseball bat, puts on a jacket and hat and leaves through the front door to seek help from her neighbor Mr. Smithy . . . .

## ACT 7

## MAXWELL SNEAKS SMITHY
## INTO HIS ROOM

**Scene 1.**

**MAXWELL** . . . . (He quietly opened his back door. Speaking softly to Smithy) . . . Come on Smithy, come! Come!

**SMITHY** . . . . (He answered softly) OK, Ok I am coming . . . . (as he followed Maxwell into his bedroom)

**MAXWELL** . . . OK, step in there. (As he showed him the closet) And don't you make a sound, you old fart. (as they both giggled softly)

**SMITHY** . . . . (Stepped in and made himself comfortable as he whispered). Boy! oh boy! (as he closed the door of the closet)

**MAXWELL** . . . (He returned through the rear door that they both entered and makes his way to the front when he heard his wife returning from Mr. Smithy's house. He hid behind the bushes as he looked at his beautiful wife as she entered through the door)

**Suzette** . . . . (On entering her living room as she called out to her kids) Marvin, Sue, you can both come out now. (as she sat down on the couch with both her hands on her face, sadly looking straight ahead)

**MARVIN AND SUE** . . . . (They nervously ran to their mothers side with concern)

**MARVIN** . . . . (He asked his mother) Well Momma, what happened at Mr. Smithy's house? (he puts his arms around his mother's neck)

**SUZETTE** . . . . Mr. Smithy was not home, and his wife said, that Mr. Smithy had not been home for the last three days . . . . (she now begins to sob) . . . .

**SUE** . . . . (She sat next to her mom) Please Mom don't cry we can still go and search for daddy, I am not afraid.

**MARVIN** . . . Yes, Momma, come on let's go, I am not afraid either . . . .

**SUZETTE** . . . . Okay, let me go and pack some warm clothes for your father, he might be all cold and shivering out there in that cold weather. (She leaves and goes into her bedroom to get some clothes to take along)

MEANWHILE SUE AND MARVIN WAS FUSSING ABOUT THEIR FATHER'S WELFARE . . . .

**SUE** . . . (Saying to Marvin) My daddy is a boxer, no-one can hurt him . . .

**MARVIN** . . . Yea, who say so, if a few bad men jumps him, what do you think will happen to him? They can kill him, boxer or not, he will be dead for sure, silly you. (as he pushed her away from him)

**SUE** . . . (When Marvin said those words of her father dying, she burst out a loud scream, Mommy! Mommy! (as she called out for her mother.) Marvin said my daddy is dead. (She is crying and tapping her feet on the floor in anger.

**SUZETTE** . . . . (Heard her daughter screaming, quickly rushed out from her room . . . . What is it? What is it? (she rushed to her daughter's side)

**MAXWELL** . . . . (Returning from his hiding spot and was getting ready to enter into the front door also heard Sue's screaming, as he dashed in the midst of them saying). What is it? What is the matter? (they all began looking at each other with bewilderment) . . .

**SMITHY** . . . . (Also heard the screaming of Sue, rushed in with a golf stick in his hands raised over his head, ready to strike if needed.) What is it? What is wrong? What is happening? . . . (He stopped in the midst like everyone else, everyone looking at each other wandering what is going on)

**SUE** . . . Oh, Daddy,! oh Daddy,! it is really you! You are not dead? You are not dead. (She held on to her daddy)

**MAXWELL** . . . . (He stretched out his hands to his daughter as he embraced her. And said, come here little princess, give your daddy a smooch. And who, said I was dead. (he kissed her on the cheek).

**SUZETTE** . . . . (Looking curiously at Mr. Smithy, and then at Maxwell) O.K. fellas, tell me what is going on? (As she glanced at Smithy and said,) I just came from your house Mr. Smithy and your worried wife told me you had not been home for three days, and now I saw you coming out of my bedroom,(as she glanced over at her husband and said), would some-one tell me what's going on here?

**MAXWELL** . . . . (Looked at his wife and slowly walked over to her with his out-stretched hands) I am sorry darling. (they embraced as the two kids joined them)

**SMITHY** . . . . (Standing there all puzzled and looking at the kids said,) May I have something to drink, with all this excitement taking place here, I need something to calm me down.?

**SUE** . . . (Looked at Smithy,) Yes sir, you can. (as she hurried to the kitchen and returned with a glass of water.) Thank you replied Smithy, standing there nervously looking at Suzette.

**SUZETTE** . . . . OK fellas, let us calm down and chat a little. Something is fishy with you both,(She looked over at Smithy) and you sir, your wife told me you had been missing for three days. Where had you been? And what had you been doing? Your pretty wife at home is so worried about you. (pointing her fingers at him)

**MAXWELL** . . . . OK sweetheart, give the guy a break, he saved my life out there tonight.

**SUZETTE** . . . . Oh, honey, (as she now carefully looked at her husband) Your lips, they are busted, and your face it is bruised. Oh my Lord. What happened?

**SUE** . . . . (Left and brought another glass of water and gave it to Mr. Smithy) Here you are sir, another glass of cold water to calm you down. (she giggled)

**SMITHY** . . . Thank you little princess. (he took the glass of water and drank it down, he glanced at Maxwell, as he signals him to tell his story to his wife).

**MAXWELL** . . . . (He blinked his eyes at Smithy and took his wife's hands as he gently kissed his wife on her cheek and said softly to her) I have something to say to you . . . .

**SUZETTE** . . . . (She smiled at him and said,) Yes and I already know what you are going to tell me.

**MAXWELL** . . . (Smiling back at her) Yep. Yep. So you already know, eh? Wow, my wife is a prophet, hey kids your mommy is a prophet.

**SUE** . . . (Looking at her dad and asked) A Prophet! What is prophet? (looking curiously at her mother)

**MAXWELL** . . . . Well, my princess, a prophet is someone who can tell and predict the future like no-one else for example, men such as Isaiah, Ezekiel, or better yet Jeremiah. Those men were called prophets because they were gifted men of God and so the people listened to them.

**SUE** . . . Hey Dad, so you mean mommy has gifts like those men. She is a prophet. (still looking at her mom)

**MAXWELL** . . . . (He called over his daughter and his son to him) Hey, kids come over here, Daddy have something to tell Mommy and Mr. Smithy is here to witness me telling her this news.

**SUZETTE** . . . . (Interrupted again, honey it is alright-you don't have to tell me. You have lost my diamond-earrings or they beat you up and took them away, it is alright, you are alive, I can get more jewelry any time, but a handsome and loyal man is very hard to find. (she hugged him and kissed him as teardrops rolled down her cheeks). You are safe my love. (as she turned to Smithy) Thanks, thanks Smithy for taking care of my Max. (The kids went and hugged Mr. Smithy.)

**MAXWELL** . . . . (Sitting close to her wiped her eyes and said) I love you honey, and I am so sorry about your precious diamond-earrings They have been with us so long. (he kisses her on the fore-head)

**SMITHY** . . . (Stunned and amazed by Suzette's remarks of her precious diamond gold earring said to her,) I am indeed very pleased and happy for you. If, only my wife was not so materialistic, I would be a happy man like my friend here, now if I had lost such a valuable piece of jewelry, she will probably lock me out of my house and divorce me in a wink of an eye. Anyway (as he now glanced at Maxwell, picked up the bag that he had with him and emptied out it's contents. The lofty sum of money fell onto the floor)

**SUZETTE** . . . . (She cried out) Oh mercy! where did you get all that money? (she quickly got up and began picking up the bills, as the kids also joined in the fun.)

**SMITHY AND MAXWELL LOOKING AT EACH OTHER WITH A BIG SMILE ON THEIR FACES AS THEY LOOK AT HIS FAMILY PLAYS WITH THE MONEY- . . . .**

**SUZETTE** . . . . (Stopped handling the money returning to Maxwell's side on the couch and asked) So, um, will someone tell me what we looking at lying in the middle of our floor? (pointing to all the money)

**MAXWELL** . . . . Well, this morning, on my way to town, I met Smithy sitting on the bench outside at the bus-stop. So we chat for awhile and he decided to travel with me to town, since we have not been together for awhile.

**SUZETTE** . . . . Yes, that is good, two old buddies together again, I could imagined what fun you both probably had? (she looked at him with a sly expression on her face) I could only imagined, hah, hah ho (she laughed)

**SMITHY** . . . . (Interrupted) Oh, no, no Mrs. Max, it is not what you are implying here. Maxwell nearly lost his life, look at him, do think we were having fun in his condition? Oh no, not at all, it is only luck or some type of blessing in disguise that I came to win this amount of money. (he glanced over at Maxwell)

**MAXWELL** . . . . Yes, Smithy is telling the truth when we entered the beginning of the town there were lots of activities., merchants and vendors, music, food, people shopping and partying on the streets. Well, I saw some strange looking wrist-watches, so I began browsing around looking at them,

**SMITHY** . . . Yep, as Maxwell went into the store looking at the different types of watches, I noticed on the other side of the street a chartered bus with a sign read which **Free ride to the horse-racing track today**. Well, (as he chuckled) Max, you remember our young days, ha. Hah. So I got in and it took off. I was lucky, it was there that I have won all this money $25,000.00 thousand dollars. (he began laughing) ha, ha, ho ho, (he looked at Maxwell, as he too began laughing).

**SUZETTE** . . . (Suzette looked at both of them and soon she too began laughing), hah, hah, ho, ho. And then everyone is laughing as. SUE AND MARVIN STILL PLAYING WITH THE MONEY BEGAN LAUGHING.

**SUZETTE** . . . . (She stopped laughing and asked Smithy) So my dear Mr. Smithy, I had gone over to your home to see if you were there so you could have gone with us to look for Maxwell, when your wife told me you had been missing for three days. (she looks at him suspiciously and said) were you in our bedroom closet all those days, eh. eh? (as she punched him jokingly on his chest.)

**SMITHY** . . . (He quickly got up and replied) Hey, wait, just wait here a second. It is not like that. It is not what you are thinking I am not a peeping tom.

Hey Maxwell, please explain to Suzette about this arrangement.

SUZETTE . . . (Now looked at her husband sitting at her side) What arrangement, darling I want to hear this, (she chuckled)

MAXWELL . . . . After Smithy left me I got into a fight with the Zebra gang, and a few other rough situations, at one incident I fell down on a platform and fainted . . . . A merchant fellow revived me, after fighting with the Zebra Gang they took the things I had bought to bring home. I had given up on patience and so I decided to call it quits and try to make it back home, beaten, hungry, thirsty, I found a bench and lied down, tired and hurting. (The kids surrounded their dad as they listened with compassion and concerned)

SMITHY . . . . (Still standing looking at Maxwell) Max is right, I found him lying on this bench groaning in pain and drops of blood running down his face. I was shock and frightened, I cleaned him up and on the way here we made a deal and a promise to one another, after he told me his ordeal, of losing your diamond-earring, I said him, because of you I had a chance to win this money, for the past week, I have been going to the race track and never won anything, so I told him, I will split with him half of this money, if you did not get mad or angry with him for losing your diamond earrings.

**SUZETTE** . . . (Bewildered and astonished, listening without saying a sound, looking and smiling at Maxwell) ah, ha, ah ha. Ok, ok (shaking her head)

**MAXWELL** . . . . Well, the plan was for him to hide in our bedroom, I was to take you into the bedroom and give you the bad news of losing your diamond-earrings without the kids around, and if you did not scream, cussed me out or getting mad with me, he will share his winning. So that was the reason why he was in our closet, and, I put him in there, so it is not what you were insinuating about his characteristic qualities OK, my love? (He kissed her on the cheeks as she blushes)

**SMITHY** . . . . (He stepped towards her and stretched out his hands and shook Suzette's hands and said) You are a marvelous woman, it is my pleasure to share my winning with such fine neighbors. And to you my friend Maxwell, you have won a good bet. Suzette never once felt mad or angry about losing her precious diamond-earrings. She posses the power of patience. (He looked down at the kid still playing with the money. They began to divide up the money. When he said to Maxwell) Keep the money here, in the morning 1 shall return with my wife so we can celebrate.

**MAXWELL and SUZETTE** . . . . (Got up from their couch, shook his hands, gave him a big hug) Hey buddy, thanks, see you in the morning, Goodnight. (Smithy said goodbye to the kids and left.)

**MAXWELL** . . . (Looking at his kids as they are separating the big bills from the small bills softly said to them) O.K. little ones, daddy kept you up too late already, and thanks for getting ready to rescue me, come we must go to bed now, in the morning we will celebrate some more. (He looked at Marvin and said,) Thanks Marvin, it looks like your prayers was a success, now you can have any amount of meat on your plate, how is that big guy? (he goes and hugged his son)

**MARVIN** . . . . (Hugging his dad as he answered) Yes, Daddy and now you can have more slices of toast and lots of coffee, ha, ha, (as he too laughed and went to their bed rooms) Goodnight, Daddy and l am happy you are back, goodnight Mom.

**SUZETTE** . . . (Standing holding Maxwell's hands) Goodnight Marvin, Goodnight Sue.

**SUE** . . . . (She finally got up from counting the money and says) Daddy, we are rich now, ain't we.!

**MAXWELL** . . . . (Hugged her) Yes my little princess, now your mommy and I will be spending lots of time with you and Marvin, now hurry off to bed, Marvin is already in his bed.

**SUE** . . . O.K. Daddy, goodnight(as she stretched her hands upwards for him to bend down so she can kiss him before going to her bedroom)

**SUZETTE** . . . (Both remaining there in the living room, holding hands as they look at each other and smile, they slowly embrace each other as their lips met when she whispered into his ear) I feel another earthquake coming on, this time it is going to be a big shake, Isn't Max? (They both began giggling as they got up and went to their room and shut the door . . . .

# ACT 8

## THE SURPRISE REWARD.

**Scene. 1.**

THE AWFUL NIGHT IS OVER WITH ALL THE EXCITEMENTS WITH THE RETURN OF MAXWELL AND SMITHY. IT IS ABOUT 8:00 AM IN THE MORNING. BIRDS ARE FLYING AROUND WHISTLING THEIR FAVORITE TUNES, THE NEIGHBORS' DOGS ARE BARKING AWAY. A PLEASANT BREEZE IS BLOWING, IT IS SATURDAY MORNING. THE WEEKEND BEGINS . . . .

**MAXWELL** . . . . (Is sitting on his front porch, looking towards his friend Smithy's house reading his morning news-paper. His wife entered out from the house and gave him a hot cup of coffee). Thanks honey, I am wondering, where is Smithy? You think he is alright? He should have been here already with all of his money lying in our dinning room floor.

**SUZETTE** . . . (She sat down beside him) Well, I do hope so, having won all that money at the race track, she should be a very happy woman she giggled) I am happy, ain't you?

**MAXWELL** . . . . Yes my darling but she is not you. Some people are never satisfy with their accomplishments, they complain all the time, and that is his wife. But, I must admit to you he claims, he loves his wife very much with all her complaining (he turned and kissed his wife on her cheek)

**SMITHY** . . . . (Is heard as he was whistling his favorite tune coming from his home.)

**MAXWELL** . . . . Listen! listen, it is Smithy. (Maxwell began whistling the same tune, he got up and strolled towards the whistling sounds of his friend Smithy)

**SUZETTE** . . . also got up and took a few steps with her husband towards the sound and stop.

**SMITHY** . . . . (Heard the whistling sound and paused his whistling for a second, then he started once more as Maxwell continued to returned his whistling sounds. He saw Maxwell and his wife as they are waving at him, he called out). Hey, guys, what a beautiful, sunny morning with this cool wind blowing through? (he greeted them, he gave Suzette a hug, he shook Maxwell's hands) How are you feeling Max boy, still hurting from all that whipping those bastards put on your ass? (he laughed) ha, ha, ho, ho, hee, hee . . . .

**MAXWELL** . . . . Hey, watch your mouth! anyway, thanks, pal, my beautiful wife fixed me up and then gave me a soothing massage, and boy that healed all my wounds. (laughing) hah, hah. hoo, hoo. (puts his arm around Suzette when he uttered those words)

**SUZETTE** . . . . (Looking keenly at Smithy) So how did you make out last night? Was your wife angry with you for finally showing up after three days?

**SMITHY** . . . . Well, when l got home last night, she was asleep and so I did not wake her up, she gets very mad, so I gave her a kiss on her forehead and went to sleep.

**MAXWELL** . . . But, how about this morning? Is she still sleeping (smiling at him) come on Smithy, don't tell me that all your wife does is complain and sleep.

**SMITHY** . . . Hey buddy, you said it, now you folks understand why I do what I do to make me happy and not end up in some body's mad house. ha, ha, (laughing, laughing). Come on let's go inside and play with all our money, have a little wine and champagne with a juicy steak and l lobster tails to blend in, hah, hah, hah, (he winked at Maxwell and heads for the door)

**MAXWELL** . . . (puts his arms around his neck) Hey buddy, you're my friend.

**SUZETTE** . . . . O.K. Fellas, lets go into the house and get this party started (as she followed). Listen up, you big winners both of you will have to go to the super market if we are to celebrate and plan our goals for retirement, ha, hah, ho(she giggled) we have no groceries left.

**MAXWELL** .... Is it that bad Suzette?

**SUZETTE** .... Yes, Maxwell, it was that serious, but God is good, He is an awesome God, He looks out for his faithful believers and children.

**SMITHY** .... (Goes over where he left his money) Hey Max, the money is still lying here from last night, (pointing down at the lump sum and looking at Maxwell).

**SUZETTE** .... Well, where do you expect it to be? Under our bed or closet? Ha, ha, (she laughed)

**SMITHY** .... (Also laughed) Nay. nay. It's o.k. so come close Maxwell, let's divide up our funds here as we agreed.

**SUZETTE** .... O.K. Let me make us some coffee. How about that?

**SMITHY** .... Thanks Suzette, I could use a nice hot cup of coffee.

**MAXWELL** . . . . (Getting down on the floor as they begun counting out the money and make two piles, when suddenly he heard a car horn blowing outside of his house, he quickly got up and goes outside).

**SMITHY** . . . . Quickly took off the covering from the couch and covered his money lying on the floor saying). I'll be back Mr. money) chuckles and followed Maxwell outside).

**SUZETTE** . . . . (Heard the sounds of the car horn also rushed outside at the side of Maxwell) What is it? What is it? (a bit nervous and frightened)

**MARVIN AND SUE** . . . . (Also rushed out on the porch in their pajamas beside their parents looking on with concern and fear as they clung unto their parent's hands) Mommy! Mommy! Daddy! Daddy (as they cried out.).

**A POLICE VEHICLE IS IN FRONT OF THEIR HOUSE. TWO POLICE-OFFICERS DRESSED IN THEIR UNIFORMS GOT OUT.**

**1st Officer** . . . . (Looking at the folks standing on the porch) Good morning folks, what a wonderful day? Hello youngsters . . . .

**MAXWELL** . . . . Good-morning to you too sir, and yes it is a beautiful day. What can we do for you officer sir?

**1ˢᵗ officer** . . . . We are looking for a certain fellow by the name of Maxwell. And the citizens down the street told us that you might be able to help us.

**SUZETTE** . . . . (Stepping forward) Yes, we can and may I asked what you want with this fellow? Is he in some kind of trouble?

**2ⁿᵈ Officer** . . . . (Slowly stepped over to his partner's side) No madam. We are here to present to him a certificate of good citizenship and a reward of $10,000.00 dollars for his single handed fighting with the most vicious gang in our city zone. The whipping Mr. Maxwell put on those guys cause one of them to have medical treatment, and on that visitation to the medical facility we were able to apprehend the leader and all of it's members.

**1ˢᵗ Officer-.** Yes, Madam, they told us about this fellow who fought them, seems like a retired boxer and so after investigating the facts we got the information from your kinsfolk.

**MAXWELL AND SMITHY AS THEY BEGAN STARING AT EACH OTHER, THEN AT THE OFFICERS** . . . .

**MAXWELL** . . . . (Now answers) Sir, I am Maxwell, yes I was a professional boxer many years ago, but after I met my lovely wife and have these two wonderful kids, I gave up boxing.

**2nd Officer** . . . . Good for you Mr. Maxwell, having a beautiful lady as her, I myself would have done the same.

**1st Officer** . . . . Well sir, since we found the person we are looking for, it is the time to present the reward check of $10,000.00 dollars and your certificate of outstanding citizen's award plaque.

**2nd Officer** . . . . (Gets the camera and takes the picture of the presentation of Maxwell and 1st officer) O.K. now how about a picture with all of you?

**SMITHY . . . . SUZETTE . . . . MARVIN . . . . SUE . . . . MAXWELLL . . . . AND 1ST OFFICER ALL POSED FOR THEIR PICTURES TO BE TAKEN** . . . .

**MAXWELL** . . . . (Amazed and filled with joy replied,) Thank you very much officers. (he hugged his wife and his two kids . . . .

**1st Officer** . . . (Goes to the car and returned with a box gift wrapped and said) we have a special surprise gift for your lovely wife.(glancing over at Suzette whom is standing alongside her husband smiling.

**SUZETTE** . . . . (Letting go of her husband's hand) A surprise gift for me? (her face lit up, her eyes opened up wide, excitements fill the air . . . (The kids, all happily prancing around in their pajamas . . . . Smithy all amazed just calm and looking on with smiling faces Maxwell holding unto his plaque and $10,000.00 dollar check, slowly stepped forward to receive her gift.

**1st Officer** . . . . But the 1st officer ignored his out stretched hands and kindly gave the wrapped package to Suzette and said) We have discovered a precious gift from the gang members and found out that there is a small inscription as to the previous owners.

**SUZETTE** . . . . (Nervously with excitement takes the gift from the officer's hand) Thank you sir, (looking quickly at Maxwell then back to the little gifted package)

**MAXWELL** . . . . (Also very much excited said,) Open it darling, open it so we can see what it is inside.

**SUZETTE** . . . . Yes! yes, I will but I already know what's inside it is my pair of diamond-earrings. Yes, yes. It is my great, great, great grand-ma's diamond-earrings! (as she began to sob and cry out loudly) Oh Momma, oh Momma! As tears rolled down her cheeks.)

**MAXWELL** . . . (Standing there looking on solemnly slowly stepped across to where his wife was standing crying and embraced her) OK, baby, it is alright, don't cry, please don't cry.

**2nd Officer** . . . . Well folks, we thank you for your time, and good luck to all of you, and the lady is right it is her grand-mother's diamond-earrings according to the craving inside of it.

**SMITHY** . . . . (Shouts out) Wow ! Wow! We are rich, Maxwell. My friend professional boxer, hey kids did you know your daddy was a fighter, hah, hah. wow !wow! My friend a boxer . . . .

**MAXWELL** . . . . Alright, alright Smithy, calm down, don't you see how emotional my wife is. Take it easy man! give her time to embrace her precious gift, even though she had not shown her emotion on my part of losing it, she had enough patience in not revealing her anger in me, love for me was more precious then, than those diamond-earrings but now it is like the prodigal son. The son returned home and the father was filled with joy, he made a big party, killed the fattest cow and invited everyone around why? Because he claimed that his son who was lost was lost is now found. They celebrated, so come on we too should celebrate for my wife's diamond-earrings has been found which was lost and which was very precious and sentimental to her. I think we should celebrate, what says my crew? (The kids hugging their mom and weeping with her. Let her hands loose and yell, Yes! Yes! Let us celebrate . . . .

**SUZETTE** . . . . (Wiping her tears away) Sorry folks, I was a little emotional there for a moment. Come let us go into the house. (they quickly followed. She goes and sat down at the table as she opened the wrapped package. She picked up the box and showed it to Maxwell.) Look Max, the same box.

**MAXWELL** . . . . (Goes over and took up the box and solemnly looked at the box as tears gather in his eyes and rolled down his cheeks) Oh darling, My dearest, I am so thrilled and happy that your mama's diamond-earrings are back with you. (he took it out of the box) Come here, let me see your right side ear, (he puts on one side) now let me see your other side, (he puts on the other side) O.K. I make a solemn pledge today within this family and my friend that we will never ever take these diamond-earrings off my darling wife's ear to take to the market again. (he then kissed her on the lips, as everyone clapped their hands and shouted Hoorah! Hoorah, Cheers, cheers! (all began laughing) Ha . . . ha . . . ha, ha . . .

**SMITHY** . . . . OK, Max and Suzette, I will be right back, I have some stuff at my house, kids get dress we are going to celebrate! (as he ran out the door)

**MARVIN** . . . . Let us go and get dress Sue! (taking his sister by her hands and went to their room)

**MAXWELL AND SUZETTE IS AT THE TABLE SITTING DOWN HOLDING HANDS . . . . SHE DRIED AWAY HIS TEAR-DROPS.**

**SUZETT**E . . . . Max, I love you very much, more than my Grandma's jewelry, no materialistic items will turn my love from you. (she kissed him on the lips)

**MAXWELL** . . . . And l love you the same my darling. (he took up his $10,000.00 check and said to her) and to my special lady, another gift for portraying the power of patience, this check of $10.000.00 dollars.

**SUZETTE** . . . . (Took the check, looked at it, smiled and kissed him on his cheek) Thanks my love. Come let us get ready for a party. (as she dance off to the living room and turned on the radio to a disco beat . . . .

**MAXWELL** . . . (Hurried to her side as he held her and began dancing the bump)

**MARVIN AND SUE NOW RUSHED IN WITH THEIR NEW CLOTHES AND BEGAN**

## JUMPIMG AROUND DANCING WITH THEIR PARENTS . . . .

**SMITHY** . . . . (Now entered with a grocery bag filled with drinks and food when he shouts) aaah! Aaah! Wow! wow !hoa! hoa . . . let the music play . . . . (as he twists and danced towards the table, put the bag down, took out a bottle of champagne, and says to Maxwell) Hey, Max, where are the glasses?

**MAXWELL** . . . (Stopped dancing, goes to the kitchen, reached into the cupboard, took out six glasses and put them down on the table) Here are the glasses Smithy!

**SMITHY** . . . . (Opened the bottle of champagne goes to the table and began to pour into the glasses, when he said to Maxwell) Max, Max, there are five of us here, who is the sixth glass for ?

**MAXWELL** . . . (Goes over to the table) Oh, Smithy, the sixth glass is for our invisible friend and our angel who protects us in our daily activities.) He pats Smithy on his shoulders, O.K. everyone, gather around, gather around, a toast, a toast . . . . yea, yea, yea yah O.k. who will go first?

**SUE** . . . . (Raised her hands) Me, me, I want to go first Daddy.

**MAXWELL** . . . . Alright princess, you begin . . .-

SUE . . . .(She raised her glass to toast when her dad looked at her raising her glass)

**MAXWELL** . . . . Hold it princess, pour some of that liquid in my glass. (he extended his hand with his glass to his daughter as she poured some of her champagne into her father's glass and giggled . . . .

**SUE** . . . . O.K. Daddy(she poured some of her champagne into her dad's glass) Alright, first I want to thank God for taking care of my daddy and for bringing him back safely to us and thank God for my Daddy beating up those bad guys . . . . yea . . . . yea . . . . (she lifts up her glass) yea, yea to my Daddy(As they all sipped their champagne.)

**MARVIN** . . . . My turn. Well l want to thank Mr. Smithy for finding and helping my Daddy home and for sharing his money that he won at the race track with us . . . . yea, yea, yea (they all toast)

**SUZETTE** . . . . O.K. and, here is to my wonderful and dedicated husband in the whole wide world and to Mr. Smithy his long-time school buddy for many years, may our friendship last forever, yea, yea, yea. (they toast)

**SMITHY** . . . . (He reaches over to the bottle of champagne, takes it up and says) We need more champagne in our glasses. (he poured some into Maxwell's and Suzette's glass . . . .

**MARVIN** . . . . (.Puts his glass out for more when Smithy looked at him and shook his head)

**SMITHY** . . . . (Looks at Marvin) Sorry young man, you have enough in your glass, you don't need any more. (As he winked at his parents). Al-right, here is my toast to the most wonderful family in the whole wide world, ha, ha, ha. Yes, to Suzette by your proof to me and by the power of patience and because you remained humble and faithful and not adoring material items, our God has rewarded you more then you were expecting. And my dear friend Maxwell, it is because of you today we can celebrate such an honor of a little wealth and your devoted friendship to my family . . . . yeh! yeh! yeh . . . . But wait a moment . . . there is a knocking at the door . . . . **At the door** . . . . knock, knock, knock . . . .

**Maxwell** . . . . (Raised his hands for silence . . . . looked at Smithy who stopped speaking . . . . Then he said to the kids . . . . Go and see who is at the door please . . . .

**Both Kids** . . . . Looked at their father and went to the door and opened it as they both yelled out loudly . . . . **Auntie Smithy, Auntie Smithy** (As they held unto Smithy's wife hands who slowly walked in . . . . (a dashing hairdo, fancy out fit and jewelries all pretty up and said out loudly . . . . **Smithy' s Wife** . . . . Well, let's get on with the party, don't look at me (as they all embraced each other and began celebrating as the piles of dollars lying on the floor . . . .

**Suzette;** (Hi, girl, where have you been hiding with that fine body of yours?. Look at all that money, girl we have some traveling and partying to do with our family . . . come on let's dance . . . . (as they got down)

**MAXWEL and SMITHY**: They are shocked and surprised as they nodded at each other to join their wives in the celebration . . . . They joined their wives dancing around the pile of money. They began picking up the dollar bills and throwing them into the air as they laughed, and laughed and danced around the room . . . .

Meanwhile Marvin is seen sneaking at the table as he poured some more champagne into his glass. He now joined the party . . . . dancing, singing and laughing with his sister and parents . . . . ha ha ho (THE CURTAIN CLOSES).

## THE END.